Totally Cute Puppies

This book belongs to...

Ticktock

An Hachette UK Company
www.hachette.co.uk

First published in the USA in 2015 by Ticktock,
an imprint of Octopus Publishing Group Ltd
Carmelite House, 50 Victoria Embankment
London, EC4Y 0DZ
www.octopusbooks.co.uk
www.octopusbooksusa.com
www.ticktockbooks.com

Distributed in the US by
Hachette Book Group USA
1290 Avenue of the Americas
4th and 5th Floors
New York, NY 10020

Distributed in Canada by
Canadian Manda Group
664 Annette Street
Toronto, Ontario, Canada M6S 2C8

ISBN 978 1 78325 225 1
Printed and bound in China
1 3 5 7 9 10 8 6 4 2

Written by Mandy Archer   Designed by Doch & Doris Design and Development Ltd
Creative Director: Miranda Snow   Managing Editor: Karen Rigden
Production Controller: John Casey   US Editor: Jennifer Dixon

Picture Credits

Every effort has been made to trace the copyright holders, and we apologize in advance for any unintentional omissions.
We would be pleased to insert the appropriate acknowledgement in any subsequent edition of this publication.

istockphoto.com alvarez 57 br; Fenne 10 al; happyborder 10 ct; jenek222 13 bl; Liliboas 70 m; lilul3 24 m;
Mat Hayward 18 ct; photopix 15 m
Shutterstock Amber Williams 53 br; AnetaPics 12 cl, 37 bl, 40 b; Annette Shaff 20 l, 64 bc, 75 c, 77 br; ANP 75 b ct; Antonio
Gravante 9 al, 64 ar; Cheryl E. Davis 62 cr; chloe7992 56 bl; Christopher P Bamber 64 br; cynoclub 38 bl, 39 bl; dezi 4 m, 5 m;
Dusan Po 10 cr; Elena Dijour 64 bl; Eric Isselee 20 cr, 22 bl, 23 bl, 30 l, 30 r, 31 l, 31 r, 45 bl, 56 r, 57 bl, 66 a, 66 bc, 74 cr,
74 bc, 74 br, 75 a, 78 ar; Erik Lam 21 bc, 45 br, 47 a, 56 al, 57 al, 57 ar; Ermolaev Alexander 17 l, 53 bc, 53 bl, 67 br; GlOck 78 br;
Grisha Bruev 14 m; Helga Esteb 53 ar; HelleM 49 al; iadams 63 c; iko 42 m; IrinaK 67 ct; Ivonne Wierink 1 m; Janelle Lugge 43 m; Javier
Brosch 29 br, 38 ar, 75 bc, 75 bl; Joca de Jong 10 r; JStaley401 10 ar, 61 m, 71 m; Karramba Production 6 ct; Khoroshunova Olga
34 m; Ksenia Raykova 6 ar; Larry Maurer 12 al; lenetstan 21 ar; Lenkadan 13 bc; Lex-art 77 bl; Lilia Beck 7 ar; Liliya Kulianionak 6 br, 51
m; 65 bl; Linn Currie 25 m; Mat Hayward 7 cr, 13 ac, 65 al; Mila Atkovska 7 al; Monika Wisniewska 12 bl; Morten Normann Almeland 8 ar;
natrot 62 br; Nikolai Pozdeev 19 br; npine 66 c; Paul Matthew Photography 18 br, 32 a; Pavel Hlystov 17 r; PCHT 10 bl, 49 bl; Phil Date
38 al, 39 al; Photobac 45 ar; pixshots 33 br; poutnik 48 a; PozitivStudija 35 m; Raisa Kanareva 18 ar; rebeccaashworth 36 ar, 36 bl;
Rita Kochmarjova 37 al, 60 m, 64 al, 65 ar; Robynrg 21 br, 38 cl, 38 br, 67 ar; RoJo Images 68 cr, 69 ar, 69 bl; Scott Bolster 10 br;
Soloviova Liudmyla 65 ac; stepmorem 65 bc; Subbotina Anna 39 ct; Susan Schmitz 20 ct; tobkatrina 53 ac; Utekhina Anna 20 r; verca
65 br; Viorel Sima 7 bl, 39 ar, 80 br; Vitaly Titov & Maria Sidelnikova 26 a, 26 ar, 26 cr, 26 br, 29 bl; Vivienstock 48 b; Vlad Ageshin
49 br; VladisChern 55 br; Volkova 29 ar; Volodymyr Burdiak 13 al; Waldemar Dabrowski 64 ac; WilleeCole Photography 19 ar, 22 ar,
31 bl, 39 br, 41 b, 74 bl, 75 ct; WitthayaP 22 al; Zaretska Olga 75 cr
Thinkstock Dorottya@Mathe 3 bc; Mark Herreid 37 cr; Adam Edwards 76 br; adogslifephoto 41 a; Brian McEntire 40 a; c-foto 44
bl; cynoclub 17 cl, 21 ac, 32 ar, 33 al, 76 ar; DAJ 77 ar; Dix© 44 br; Ed Phillips 17 cr; Eric Isselee 32 bl, 32 br, 33 al; feedough 44 al;
geargodz 27 ar, 27 ac, 27 bc, 27 br; GlobalP 28 ar, 28 bl, 29 c, 46 ar, 62 ar, 74 al, 74 ac; Ingram Publishing 76 bl;
John Mcallister 74 ar; Jupiterimages 29 al; Katrina Brown 12 cr; Liza Barry 50 m; lucato 78 bl; Mapoula 9 br; monels 76 al;
nickpo 8 bl; Purestock 9 bl; ronibgood56 77 m; Silense 32 al, 44 ar; timaj 33 cr, 47 b; WesAbrams 78 al;
WilleeCole 29 bc, 33 ar, 45 al, 74 c; YekoPhotoStudio 28 al

Totally Cute Puppies

Contents

Too Cute!

Who let the dogs out?

CHAPTER 1

Doggie Delights

Do you love puppies? From the poshest pedigree to the messiest mutt in the park, pups are furry, friendly, and love to play! Whether you're a proud pet owner or your head is full of doggy daydreams, your animal adventure starts here...

Barking Brilliant!

What makes a dog such a special pet?

They are man's best friend. Dogs are sociable animals that soon become devoted to their owners. The newspapers and Internet are full of stories of pups making heroic rescues to save people.

No matter where you've been or what you've done, your dog will always be pleased to see you when you come home. It's impossible to look at a pup's waggy tail and not smile!

Puppies and dogs come in all kinds of wonderful shapes and sizes. Every breed has its own unique coloring, features, and characteristics.

Living with a doggy keeps us cheerful. Research has officially proved that people with pet pups are happier than those without.

Dogs can sniff out all kinds of yummy and yucky smells. Inside their noses there are an incredible 220 million scent cells. Some dogs, like beagles, have many more.

Pups are superplayful! They can't help rolling in muddy puddles, chewing socks, and running after balls.

Many dogs have jobs. Some help blind people, while others are trained by the police to track scents. Other breeds work on farms, rounding up sheep.

They also go bananas at the sight of a leash or the mention of a walk!

Dogs keep you safe. Most will try and guard their home, barking loudly at the first sign of trouble.

They're family. Dogs like to live in packs - your pet sees those living in your house as the other members of his pack. This is what makes him so loving, loyal, and eager to hang out with you 24/7.

Pawfect Pooches

What's your top dog? There are so many breeds to choose from! Color the paw print next to the pup that you would love to pet.

Pomeranian

Cute toy dog with a full ruff of hair around its neck. Its fur grows in all sorts of colors, from creamy white to blue-black.

West Highland White Terrier

Lively pup with a thick coat of fur, short legs, and loads of personality. Perky ears, white beard, and a wet button nose.

Beagle

Long ears, big eyes, and a typically three-colored coat - it has to be a beagle! Its wiry fur protects it from thorny shrubs.

Golden Retriever

Blond pup with a people-pleasing personality. A lovable pet with a face that actually seems to smile when you walk into the room.

Great Dane

Gentle-hearted puppy that grows very, very big! Short, silky fur, enormous paws, and a long tail that tapers to a point.

Mixed Breed

Not every pup has to be a pedigree! Dogs that are a mixture of different breeds are just as beautiful.

Magical Mix-ups

Hybrid dogs are a cross between two different breeds.
Every one is unique, and these pups also have fabulous names!
Labradoodles, puggles, and cockapoos!

Mix and match!

Can you figure out these delightful doggy combinations?
Draw a line to match each name to the correct pedigree parents.

1. Maltese terrier and Yorkshire terrier

A. schnoodle

2. golden retriever and collie

B. pugapoo

3. springer spaniel and cocker spaniel

C. puggle

4. pug and beagle

D. sprocker

5. schnauzer and poodle

E. morki

6. pug and poodle

F. golli

Check your answers on page 80.

Can you dream up a brand-new doggy combination? Draw a picture of the adorable little pup, and then write its official name underneath.

by ....

At Your Service...

As well as being loyal, friendly, and impossibly cute, dogs are hard workers! Many pups have special skills and can be trained to follow signals and commands.

Search and rescue dog

The first search dogs are thought to have been St. Bernards - a huge mastiff breed from Switzerland. Nowadays, many different types help rescue travellers who are lost or injured. They also do vital work seeking out survivors in disaster areas after events such as earthquakes and avalanches.

Sheepdog

Not many farms can operate without a sheepdog in residence! Herding dogs like border collies are smart pups that can understand complex whistles and commands. They work with the farmer to expertly round up sheep and cattle.

Police dog

The most common police dogs are German shepherds - intelligent, brave animals that are strong enough to pin down a suspect. Some police departments prize their K-9s so highly they give them their own police badges and IDs.

Sled dog

Huskies and other sled dogs are an important form of transport in snowy Arctic regions. They work in teams to pull sleds loaded with passengers, mail, and supplies. Well-trained packs also make excellent racers. Mush! Mush!

Guide dog

All across the world, thousands of guide dogs are working hard to help blind people live a normal life. Guide dogs are chosen as very young pups and trained carefully so that they stay steady, calm, and loyal to their handler at all times.

Sniffer dog

Sniffer dogs are excellent at detection. The police use them to hunt out criminals, explosives, and illegal substances. As well as having an amazing sense of smell, bloodhounds are born with a natural tracking instinct.

Other waggie workers

- Acting dog
- Hearing dog
- Military dog
- Therapy dog

Too Cute!

Yep. A hug would be good right now.

CHAPTER 2

Puppy Patrol

A pup is a friend that needs love and care forever, just like you!
It only takes a little thought and effort every day to make a pet feel
safe and content. How would you welcome a new puppy?

My Puppy Promise

Are you ready to make your puppy promise? Think carefully about what it means to be a good dog owner. If you're truly ready to be there for your furry best friend, read the pledge and sign your name at the bottom.

I promise to be kind to puppies everywhere. If I am lucky enough to have a dog come to live with me. I will give it all of the things that it needs to keep its tail wagging. Every puppy needs...

* a cozy bed
* good food

* fresh water
* walks every day

* lots of cuddles

I will do all that I can to make sure that my pup's coat stays shiny. its eyes stay smiley. and its nose stays cold and wet!

Signed ....

Write your name here.

Choosing a name for a new pup is a big decision. Will you go for something cute, funny, or unusual? Read the tips, and then write in a name for the marvelous mutts below.

Look and listen

When it comes to picking a name, you might just need to look at your pup. Does it have fluffy fur, a mischievous face, or a multicolored coat? Your pet can be a great source of inspiration!

Curly

Scamp

Patches

Keep things simple

Pups respond best to short, high-frequency sounds because they find them easiest to hear. Think about names that begin with consonants, taking care to avoid anything that could be confused with a command.

Beau

Molly

Jasper

Don't forget

Once you've decided, you will be using your dog's name a lot. Shorter names are much easier to shout when you need to call your pup back quickly.

Stella

Kyla

Cody

My fave names

Four Furry Feet

Some puppies are sweet and shy, while others are bold and barky! Every dog is different, so when you meet a new one, take the time to watch it for a while first to see how it likes to be treated.

Feeling shy

Always check with an adult before touching any dog that you don't know, as nervous pups can nip. If the pup seems unsure, help it feel relaxed by getting down on the floor alongside it and avoiding eye contact so it doesn't feel threatened.

Heavy lifting

If your pup wants to be picked up, scoop it up gently by placing your arms around its four legs and bringing it towards you. Hold the puppy close to your chest. It's your way of saying, "Relax, buddy, I've got you!"

Patted pooch

Gently stroke your pup from its head down to its tail, running your hand in the direction of the fur. Many dogs love having their ears rubbed and their tummy tickled, too.

Canine Couture

When you've really got to know your puppy, you can start having fun together! Many owners like to dress up their pets. If you decide to give it a try, always make sure that your dog is safe and comfortable.

Dress-up rules!

1. Check with an adult before you begin, and choose a costume that will allow your pet to move around freely.

2. Make sure that your puppy can see and hear properly in its costume and that there are no parts that it could chew and swallow.

3. Don't put your pet in anything that will make it overheat.

4. Only keep your puppy dressed up for a short amount of time. Don't let it roam outside with clothes on, as it could get its outfit caught.

5. Reward your pet with lots of treats for being a star. If it doesn't seem comfortable, however, take the costume off right away.

What do you think? Too much?

Cutie Quiz

What type of puppy are you? Take this quiz, and you might discover that some people and pooches have a lot in common!

1. Your favorite movies are...

A. cute chick flicks ✓

B. silly comedies

C. action-packed adventures

D. heart-warming animal tales

2. When you get to school, you head to...

A. the restroom to check your hair

B. the cafeteria to find your friends

C. the playground to play ball

D. the classroom to chill out ✓

3. The best way to describe your style is...

A. stylish with lots of bling

B. colorful and quirky

C. practical and relaxed ✓

D. trendy but not OTT

4. Your dream vacation would be...

A. shopping in New York ✓

B. having a blast at a waterpark

C. snowboarding in the Alps

D. chilling on a sandy beach

5. Your family always complains that you...

A. hog the bathroom	
B. talk over the TV	
C. jump on the sofa	✓
D. take ages to get out of bed	

6. The motto that most suits you is...

A. think big, dream bigger	✓
B. a smile makes everything better	
C. where there's a will there's a way	
D. tomorrow is another day	

Mostly As - pampered Pekingese

You're fluffy, fashionable, and always well-groomed, just like the adorable Pekingese. When they need some pedigree pampering, your friends know just who to call!

Mostly Bs - jolly Jack Russell

Have you ever played with a Jack Russell terrier? You should get along well - you're both playful, happy, and full of fun. It seems you've got a habit of turning frowns upside down!

Mostly Cs - spirited spaniel

Wow - you struggle to sit still for a minute! Cocker spaniels are just the same. You are both bouncy, excitable, and always on the go. If only everyone had as much energy as you do!

Mostly Ds - mellow mastiff

You're so laid-back, you're almost horizontal! You think the same way as a mastiff. Why rush today what could be done tomorrow, when you could take it easy instead?

Ages and Stages

Are doggy ages the same as ours? Do puppies teethe, play, and learn, just like babies? Let's take a peek at those adorable baby days.

Hello world!

A mother dog normally gives birth to a litter of up to six puppies, but she could have as many as a dozen. At first, puppies' eyes are shut. They nestle into their mom to feed and keep warm.

Waking up

After a couple of weeks, most new puppies will begin to open their eyes. Their ears open up, too. Little by little, the dogs start becoming aware of the world around them.

Eating and growing

After a month, puppies start developing teeth. A healthy young dog has a big appetite, needing at least four meals a day to grow big and strong.

First steps

By three weeks, pups will be able to walk, make yapping sounds, and wag their tails. Things suddenly start to move very quickly. Once they are mobile, puppies want to get out and explore!

Leaving the nest

Puppies aren't ready to join a new human family until at least six to eight weeks old. Up until then, they need to be near mom. As well as feeding them milk, she teaches them precious lessons about life in a pack. Now that they're ready to move on, pups are full of energy and curiosity, although they still need lots of nap time, too.

It's a Dog's Life

Dogs and puppies age at a different speed to humans. Most dogs are thought to be mature by the age of seven. Look at the chart to find out how old your pet is in doggy years.

How old?

Human Years	Small Dog Years	Medium Dog Years	Large Dog Years
1	15	15	15
2	24	24	24
3	28	28	28
4	32	32	32
5	36	36	36
6	40	42	45
7	44	47	50
8	48	51	55
9	52	58	61
10	56	60	66
11	60	65	72
12	64	69	77
13	68	74	82
14	72	78	88
15	76	83	93
16	80	87	120
17	84	92	
18	88	98	
19	92	101	
20	96		

did you know?

Dalmatians are famous for their spots, but the puppies are always pure white when they are born. The first black spots usually start to appear when the little ones are three weeks old.

Too Cute!

The best things come in small packages.

CHAPTER 3

The Chic Pack

Does your pooch have a habit of rolling in mud and paddling in ponds? It's time that it was treated to a mutt makeover! Even the hairiest hobo will enjoy being brushed and pampered.

Pampered Pooch

All puppies need pampering - as well as making their fur shine, grooming brushes out dirt and old hairs. Fur-bulous!

Beautiful bonding

Grooming is a great way to get close to your dog. The more your puppy gets used to being touched, hugged, and brushed, the more placid, trusting, and happy it will be!

Brushing basics

1 Spread an old towel on the floor, or if the weather's nice, take your puppy outside. Give it lots of reassurance so it feels calm and relaxed.

2 Use a brush first and then a comb to smooth out your puppy's fur. If you come across any knots, gently tease them out. Take care to brush only in the direction that the fur is growing.

3 Work your way all over your puppy's body, from the head down to the tail. At the beginning, keep the grooming sessions short. Over time you can brush for longer.

Bathtime Buddies

Every now and then, your dog is going to need a deep clean. When the weather's nice and your pup is happy and healthy, ask an adult to help you give it a bath.

Q **A** How often?

Every two months is more than enough. If you wash your pup too often, you risk washing out the natural oils in its fur.

Q **A** Inside or outside?

On a sunny day, outside is always best. It keeps the mess under control! If you have a small dog, however, you might be able to lift it in the bath without too much water being splashed everywhere.

Q **A** Soap or shampoo?

Never use soap on your puppy – it could irritate its skin. Use lukewarm water and special dog shampoo. Rinse the fur afterwards, taking care not to get shampoo in your pup's eyes.

Q **A** How do I dry my pup?

Wrap it in a big towel and gently rub it down. Keep your pup indoors until its fur dries completely so it doesn't catch a chill.

Woofy warning: Some dogs and puppies hate spending time in the tub. See how your pet reacts, and get an adult to help you.

Designer Dawgs

What's the latest pooch couture? Our furry fashion reporter has snapped the very latest looks from the designer dogwalks! Color the paw print next to the pup that's working it best.

Prince prints

A selfie!

Dexter

Dexter wows in the dinkiest checked shirt EVER!

Lula

When it comes to leopard print, Lula keeps things classy.

Maggie

Maggie looks so pretty in pink!

Fluffy

When it comes to bling,
Fluffy jumps right in!

Scotty

Scotty's bandana
was flown in from Paris.

Fifi

Fifi is sitting pretty in
this season's pom-pom
prom dress.

Mitzy

Mitzy is working
those woollens
so well!

Riley

Riley's patent
leather boots are
simply to die for!

Dixie

Dixie has never believed in
"less is more."

Let's Accessorize!

Leashes, collars, and coats - when you're a dog, there are so many opportunities to look claw-geous! Get your colored pencils, and then use your drawing skills to give these pooches some extra pizzazz!

1 This pup would love to sniff out a brand-new bandana. Can you draw one in?

2 Set off this adorable puppy face with a stunning new hat.

In ancient China, wealthy people carried Pekingese puppies around in the sleeves of their robes.

3 This pooch likes to make a statement. Draw a designer doggy handbag that does just that!

4 It's a bling thing! Cover this pup in bows, gold, and gemstones.

Woofy warning:
These doodles are just for fun. It's not safe for real-life doggy divas to wear jewelry. The natural look is best and it's safest, too.

Picture This

There's a line of pups at the grooming salon today! Chief groomer, Bella Bouffant, doesn't know who to see first! Help her to organize her appointments by solving this pampered pooch picture quiz.

Bella Bouffant

5064/8

1. It's all about the ears with this pup's hair. Is it a...

A. papillon

B. poodle

C. Chihuahua

D. shar-pei

2. This little pup opts for a short back and sides. Is it a...

A. fox terrier

B. miniature schnauzer

C. King Charles spaniel

D. Yorkshire terrier

3. This customer keeps things au naturel. Is it a...

A. border collie

B. Tibetan terrier

C. mixed breed

D. springer spaniel

4. One of my more outrageous styles! Is it a...

A. Pekingese

B. Tibetan mastiff

C. shih tzu

D. Chinese crested dog

What a beautiful blond!
Is it a...

A. golden retriever

B. dalmatian

C. German shepherd

D. basset hound

6. This dog's dreadlocks are totally fur-bulous! Is it a...

A. pug

B. puli

C. pointer

D. Portuguese water dog

7. Guess who takes ages under the dryer? Is it a...

A. Tibetan terrier

B. Sussex spaniel

C. Irish wolfhound

D. Welsh corgi

8. This puppy dog's fur is as soft as velvet. Is it a...

A. mastiff

B. Irish setter

C. whippet

D. Weimaraner

Check your answers on page 80.

did you know?

The bichon frise is a French and Belgian breed. Its name literally means "small, curly haired dog." Many people think that poodles have French origins, too, but they are actually from Germany.

Too Cute!

Well, I'm ready. How about you?

CHAPTER 4

Doggy Day Care

If you've had a bad day at school or you're feeling down, go and hug a pooch! Doggy pals keep us active, make us giggle, and are always up for a game. Who could ask for a better friend?

Wonderful Walks

Every dog needs exercise and playtime. Although it can't speak, it will try to tell you this in its own special way. If your pup crouches forward on its front legs and then wags its tail, it's time for fun!

Out and about

When your parents next put on their boots to go dog-walking, ask to go along, too. Your pooch will love running alongside you in a park or field or at the beach! As well as keeping your pet fit, walking is a great way for a puppy to meet new pals and learn social skills.

Fetch!

Lots of doggies could happily spend their days retrieving toys, slippers, and balls. Try throwing a ball and training your pup to wait for your command before running to fetch it. Remember to give it lots of praise at the end!

did you know?

If your dog gets warm during an energetic game in the sunshine, you may not realize it at first. Hot hounds sweat only through the pads on their feet.

Water baby?

Some pups can't resist diving into the nearest pond and paddling around in circles. Others are not so sure. Some dogs' body shapes mean that swimming is not possible, especially those with short legs, like dachshunds. Check with an adult before playing in the water with your pet.

Chew it out

Treat your pet to a rubber toy or a chew bone and they'll have hours of fun! Puppies especially enjoy chewing when their new teeth are coming in, as it helps soothe their gums. Don't be surprised if your dog runs off to a favorite hiding spot to chomp.

Hunt the Kong

Kong toys are a great way to entertain your puppy. Fill the hollow with a tasty treat, such as peanut butter or cream cheese, and then give the toy to your pet. It will spend hours trying to lick the goodies out of the center!

Dogs Do the Funniest Things

Dogs love to grin, joke, and lick your face! Here are 12 of the best hound dog howlers around...

What is the name of the greatest dog detective?

Sherlock Bones!

What did the Dalmatian say after it ate a good meal?

That hit the spot!

When is a brown dog not a brown dog?

When it is a greyhound!

What do you call a dog that's come in from the snow?

A slush puppy!

What happens when it rains cats and dogs?

You might step in a poodle!

Why don't dogs
make good dancers?

Because they
have two left feet!

What did one flea
say to the other flea?

Shall we walk or
take the dog?

How do you stop a
dog smelling?

Put a clothespin
on its nose!

What do you call a
dog magician?

How can you tell
if a dog is silly?

It chases
parked cars!

A labracadabrador!

Top Tricks

Some say you can't teach an old dog new tricks, but the opposite is true! If taught patiently and properly, you'll be amazed at the things that your pet can do.

In a spin

Stand in front of your dog, and then hold a treat up for him to see. Say the word "spin" in a gentle but clear voice, and then move the treat to one side so that your dog has to turn his head to follow it. Keep moving the treat around until he has rotated in a complete circle. When he's finished, give him a cuddle and let him eat the treat. Keep practicing this and eventually you'll be able to do it without a treat.

did you know..?

Researchers have discovered that most dogs are as clever as a two-year-old child. The brainiest breed is the border collie.

Give a paw

Sit your dog in front of you. Every time he lifts his paw, say "paw" in a happy voice and give him a tasty treat. Repeat this over and over until he starts to see the connection between your command, the action, and the treat. Once he's grasped it, save your treats for the highest lifts, always remembering to give him lots of praise.

Roll over

Kneel on the floor beside your pup, encouraging him to lie down. Take a tasty treat and hold it next to his nose so that he can sniff it. Now move the treat up and over towards the dog's shoulder, encouraging him to follow the trail with his nose. He should twist further and further until he finally flops over onto his back. Good work! Give him a big cuddle and let him eat the treat. Repeat this over and over, saying "Roll over!" in a clear voice every time.

Remember
Pup tricks are just for fun! If your pet seems tired or bored, stop for the day and let him have a rest.

Too Cute!

Look, it's not going to throw itself.

CHAPTER 5

Hangin' with My Hound

Does your pet ever look up at you with big, puppy dog eyes that are impossible to resist? Dogs are super-expressive animals - using their tails, bodies, and faces to communicate with us and each other.

Look and Listen

Puppies can't use words, but that doesn't stop them making their feelings known! Look at this picture list, and then color the paw print next to the moods you've seen your mutt display.

1

I'm feeling fine!
Body check: mouth open, eyes alert and cheerful, tail wagging.

2

Let's take five...
Body check: both eyes closed, body flat on the ground, legs relaxed.

3

Whatever's happening, count me in!
Body check: head upright, pricked ears, body tensed and ready to go.

4

Come on guys, let's play!
Body check: face eager, body crouched forward on front legs, tail wagging.

You win!

Body check: rolled onto back
with tummy showing, paws up
in front.

I'm feeling frightened.

Body check: cowering body,
ears pulled back, tail tucked
underneath.

Hmm... what's this?

Body check: walking with nose
to ground, eyes alert and
focused, tail upright.

Stand back, I'm feeling mad!

Body check: teeth bared, eyes
fixed, hackles up, body ready
to pounce.

Did you know?

When your puppy lifts its leg for the tenth time on a walk, it's
not bad manners. Going to the bathroom is just another way
that dogs communicate! Each little deposit is a calling card
that other hounds use to sniff out who's been there before.

45

Doggy Dictionary

Can you speak dawg? What do your hound's woofs, whimpers, and howls really mean? Turn to the doggy dictionary to find out, and then learn the best way to tell your pet how much you care.

Translating from dog

Barking (flat)	I'm bored
Barking (high-pitched)	Where are you? I'm worried and upset.
Barking (short and sharp)	Raise the alarm, something's going on!
Barking (deep and long)	I'm giving chase.
Growling	I'm warning you!
Howling	Shout-out to the rest of my pack/help!
Whimpering	Ouch, that hurt.
Whining	I need food/company/to go outside.
Yawn (one-off)	Hmm... I'd like a rest.
Yawn (repeated)	I'm feeling uneasy about this.

Puppy pals

Your pet pooch will be your best friend but it's important to know that they're not human - as much as they feel they are!

People love giving hugs to show affection, but puppies aren't always so sure. They are pack animals and so it's very important for them to know who is top dog at all times. If you suddenly hug a dog without getting to know it, it might think you are trying to dominate it. Its first reaction could be to run away or fight back.

If you want to show your pet that you love it, speak in a soft, slow voice (shouting or loud noises can frighten it). Sit to the side of the pup, avoiding direct eye contact. When the dog seems calm and relaxed, gently stroke its back.

Your dog can't understand as many sounds as you can, so it keeps a close eye on your body language. When you teach your pup a new command, always have a hand gesture to go with it. Having a visual sign to look for will help your pet grasp what you want it to do much more easily.

Puppies are very sensitive. Although they can't understand what you are saying, they pick up on your emotions and feelings. Sometimes you don't need any words to bond with your pet, just being together is enough.

Four-legged Friends

Ever since dogs were first trained as pets, they have been our devoted companions. What makes them so utterly special? These pages are paws-itively packed full of puppy love!

Jack London

"A bone to the dog is not charity. Charity is the bone shared with the dog, when you are just as hungry as the dog."

Mark Twain

"The dog is a gentleman; I hope to go to his heaven not man's."

Charles de Gaulle

"The better I get to know men, the more I find myself loving dogs."

Marilyn Monroe

"Dogs never bite me. Just humans."

Johnny Depp

"The only creatures that are evolved enough to convey pure love are dogs and infants."

LeAnn Rimes

"My dogs are about unconditional love. It's so wonderful to walk in the door from a long day and all they want to do is be loved and to give and give..."

Edith Wharton

"My little dog - a heartbeat at my feet."

Woodrow Wilson

"If a dog will not come to you after having looked you in the face, you should go home and examine your conscience."

Charles M. Schultz

"Happiness is a warm puppy."

Unknown

"One reason a dog can be such a comfort when you're feeling blue is that he doesn't try to find out why."

Famous people pups, too!

🐾 President Obama and his family - Bo and Sunny, Portuguese water dogs.

🐾 Ryan Gosling - George, mixed breed.

🐾 Anne Hathaway - Esmeralda, chocolate Labrador.

🐾 Hugh Jackman - Dali, French bulldog

🐾 The Duke and Duchess of Cambridge - Lupo, black cocker spaniel

Too Cute!

Take that one again. I think I blinked.

CHAPTER 6

Superstar Dogs

Puppies were born to perform! The camera loves their adorable faces, funny habits, and quirky characters. Many dogs are veterans of stage and screen - some even have their own agents!

Fluffy and Famous

As well as being the "it" accessory for A-list celebrities, lots of dogs are stars in their own right! There are a dozen canine characters hiding in this wooftastic word search. Find a pen, and see if you can sniff out each and every one.

B	K	D	P	M	A	R	T	M	E	J	C
E	A	F	O	O	D	Y	B	O	O	C	S
E	U	G	Y	S	H	X	O	Q	U	I	W
T	O	R	W	P	B	N	L	A	D	Y	G
H	L	O	Y	A	G	Y	T	Y	P	O	M
O	J	M	K	T	D	T	H	Z	T	S	L
V	Q	I	N	N	W	Y	Z	O	A	R	B
E	E	T	I	V	D	A	T	D	O	L	F
N	G	R	L	J	X	Q	K	U	X	C	J
T	L	A	S	S	I	E	R	M	P	P	H
R	I	N	T	I	N	T	I	N	V	E	H
C	H	D	M	J	F	N	V	T	E	K	D

Look carefully at the letters. The names could be running in any direction - up, down, diagonally, and even backwards!

SCOOBY DOO — Shaggy's pal and great snack-eater.

TRAMP — A scruffy mutt with a heart of gold.

BEETHOVEN — A giant St. Bernard that stars in his own movie franchise.

GROMIT — A Wallace's best friend.

DEPUTY DAWG — A deputy sheriff working at the jailhouse.

BOLT — White American shepherd dog voiced by John Travolta.

RIN TIN TIN — The first Hollywood dog star.

HOOCH — The slobbery hound that drove Turner mad.

SLINKY — Stretchy toy dachshund from *Toy Story*.

LASSIE — An American TV star that always rushed to the rescue.

LADY — Disney's elegant cocker spaniel.

TOTO — The little terrier from *The Wizard of Oz*.

Check your answers on page 80.

53

Doodle Dawgs

Could you be the next "Andy Warhowl"? Get your sketchbook and start drawing the puppy you love best.

You will need

- A photo of your dog
- A pencil
- Eraser
- White paper
- Fine black pen
- Pencil sharpener

1

The easiest way to get the shape of your pup right is to first draw a soft outline. Study your photo carefully, and then draw three circles on the page, set on an imaginary diagonal line. The top circle will be the head, the middle will form the chest, and the third marks out the legs.

2

With light, soft strokes, add lines to show where the puppy's snout, legs, and tail will be. Don't press hard – you'll want to erase the circles later.

3

Once you've got the basic shape right, use your pencil to link the circles and draw in the outline of your pup. Check your photo to make sure that you've got the shape right.

4 When you're ready, use the eraser to gently remove the circles inside the outline.

5 Draw in your puppy's features. Add the eyes, nose, and mouth, then add shape to the ears, paws, and tail. Look for details that are unique to your pet. Does it have a fluffy taill or perky ears? Put everything into your picture!

6 Use your pencil to shade your puppy's coat. Most dogs have several colors in their fur, so try layering the strokes and using thick and thin strokes to make it look like hair.

7 When you've finished shading, use a fine black pen to draw in whiskers, highlight features, and pick out details to add light and shade.

Puppy Dog Tails

We don't just love playing with our pups, we enjoy reading about them, too! Naughty, kind, funny, or heroic - books are full of unforgettable hounds! Color the paw print next to the magical mutt that is closest to your heart.

Snowy

"Snowy" in English, or "Milou" in French, dates all the way back to 1929. The little white wire fox terrier is Tintin's sidekick in Hergé's comic book series. Snowy is smart, brave, and able to understand humans.

Nana

Nana is the dog that we'd all love to have around! She is the patient and responsible Newfoundland in J. M. Barrie's *Peter Pan*. In the story, Mr. and Mrs. Darling hire Nana to care for their three children - Wendy, John, and Michael.

Spot

Eric Hill began the picture book series in 1980, which has now been translated into 60 languages! Spot is a curious yellow puppy, with a spot on his body and a brown-tipped tail.

Fang

Harry Potter's friend Hagrid is a giant of a man, and so no wonder he has a giant of a dog! In the Harry Potter books, Fang is an enormous boarhound (although in the films, he's a Neapolitan mastiff!), with a habit of slobbering all over the place.

Sweetie

The Heffley's new pet dog, Sweetie, first appears in the fourth *Diary of a Wimpy Kid* novel by Jeff Kinney. Greg would have liked to call him "Ripjaw" or "Shredder," but his mom opts for a shortened version of "Sweetheart," even though the dog is a male.

Timmy

When Enid Blyton created the *Famous Five* series, she wanted a dog to be part of the lineup. Step forward George's faithful pup, Timmy - a loyal mixed breed that loves ice cream, bones, and chasing rabbits.

Pongo and Missus

Everyone knows the *101 Dalmatians* movies, but did you know that the characters come from a book by Dodie Smith? Pongo and his wife, Missus, are the parents of a litter of 15 puppies and the adoptive mom and dad of dozens more.

Animal Antics

Snoopy, Odie, and Scooby Doo - the world is full of cartoon dogs! Use this space to design your own canine comic strip. Write the words, draw the pictures, and fill the speech bubbles.

by ....

Too Cute!

Yes, it's very cute. Can you take it back now?

CHAPTER 7

It's a Dog's Life!

Let's make every day a doggy day! Make a fur-bulous pet picture
frame, circle birthdays on the puppy calendar, pit your wits in
a head-scratching hound quiz, and then whip up a batch of
crunchy treats for your favorite furry friend.

Fur-bulous Frames

It's time to show the world how much you love your pampered pooch! Make a cute picture frame shaped like a kennel, and then put a picture of your pet inside.

You will need

- 10 popsicle sticks
- A square photo of your puppy (a drawing would work, too)
- Craft glue
- Scissors
- Old newspapers
- Poster paints
- Paintbrush
- Felt-tipped pens or stickers
- A piece of stiff cardboard
- Pencil
- Ruler
- Adhesive tape

1 Put your photo face up on a flat surface. Arrange four popsicle sticks in a square shape around it, overlapping the edges to neatly frame the picture. Next, take the photo away and put it somewhere safe, and then use craft glue to stick the popsicle sticks together. This square shape will form the basis of the picture frame.

Warning
Cutting the popsicle sticks can be quite tricky. Always ask an adult to help when using scissors.

2 Arrange two more sticks at the top of the frame so they create a roof. Glue these in place, too.

3
Glue extra sticks across the roof of the kennel. You may need to cut some of the sticks down to fit.

4
Spread out some old newspapers, and then get your paints. Carefully paint the walls and roof of your kennel frame. Use any colors that you like.

5
When the paint is dry, it's time to add some decorations. Why not use stickers or make a sign with your dog's name out of cardboard to go above the door?

6
Now you're ready to mount your pup's picture inside. Put your frame on top of a piece of stiff cardboard, and then trace around the inside square. Using a ruler, draw a square around this that is 1/4 in. (1 cm) bigger all around.

7
Following the bigger outline, cut out the cardboard square, and then carefully stick your picture in the center of it - make sure it's straight! Now run a line of glue all around the edge of the cardboard and fix it onto the back of the frame.

8
From the remaining cardboard, cut out a rectangle to make a stand for your kennel frame. Fold over a 1/4-in. (1 cm) strip at the top of the rectangle and tape this to the back of the picture. Now stand the frame up and let everyone enjoy your masterpiece!

Doggy Days

With this cute canine calendar, you'll never commit another faux-paw again! Use these pages to circle all of your family's and friends' birthdays.

JANUARY

1	2	3	4	5	6	7
8	9	10	11	12	13	14
15	16	17	18	19	20	21
22	23	24	25	26	27	28
29	30	31				

Sitting pretty in the snow!

FEBRUARY

1	2	3	4	5	6	7
8	9	10	11	12	13	14
15	16	17	18	19	20	21
22	23	24	25	26	27	28
29						

All I want for Valentine's Day is... you.

MARCH

1	2	3	4	5	6	7
8	9	10	11	12	13	14
15	16	17	18	19	20	21
22	23	24	25	26	27	28
29	30	31				

It only takes a litttle sunshine to put a spring in pup's step!

APRIL

1	2	3	4	5	6	7
8	9	10	11	12	13	14
15	16	17	18	19	20	21
22	23	24	25	26	27	28
29	30					

Fashionable furries can't wait to step out in April showers!

MAY

1	2	3	4	5	6	7
8	9	10	11	12	13	14
15	16	17	18	19	20	21
22	23	24	25	26	27	28
29	30	31				

Are you ready for some May madness?

JUNE

1	2	3	4	5	6	7
8	9	10	11	12	13	14
15	16	17	18	19	20	21
22	23	24	25	26	27	28
29	30					

June days are grrrr-eat for garden games!

JULY

1	2	3	4	5	6	7
8	9	10	11	12	13	14
15	16	17	18	19	20	21
22	23	24	25	26	27	28
29	30	31				

School's out - howl for
the holidays!

AUGUST

1	2	3	4	5	6	7
8	9	10	11	12	13	14
15	16	17	18	19	20	21
22	23	24	25	26	27	28
29	30	31				

Hot dogs stretch out in the
summer sun.

SEPTEMBER

1	2	3	4	5	6	7
8	9	10	11	12	13	14
15	16	17	18	19	20	21
22	23	24	25	26	27	28
29	30					

Fall is twice as nice when you
snuggle up with a friend.

OCTOBER

1	2	3	4	5	6	7
8	9	10	11	12	13	14
15	16	17	18	19	20	21
22	23	24	25	26	27	28
29	30	31				

Hound dogs come out to
share the Halloween fun!

NOVEMBER

1	2	3	4	5	6	7
8	9	10	11	12	13	14
15	16	17	18	19	20	21
22	23	24	25	26	27	28
29	30					

In November, there's a
puppy on every sidewalk.

DECEMBER

1	2	3	4	5	6	7
8	9	10	11	12	13	14
15	16	17	18	19	20	21
22	23	24	25	26	27	28
29	30	31				

May all your waggy
Christmas wishes come true...

did you know?

Some smart stray dogs in Russia have figured out how to
ride on the subway! They travel from station to station, to find
the busiest parts of a city. They've learned that these are the
places where they're most likely to find food.

Take a Bite

Have you been sitting up and paying attention so far? Let's find out! Get your dog's tail wagging by trying your luck at this puzzling puppy quiz. Grab a pen and check the right answers.

1. Which dog is the fastest on four legs?

- A. the spaniel
- B. the greyhound
- C. the German shepherd
- D. the bull terrier

2. Which of these foods is not dangerous to dogs?

- A. chocolate
- B. pasta
- C. raisins
- D. onions

3. Why do pups get so attached to their owners?

- A. they see them as part of their pack
- B. they like their smell
- C. they think they are their mom or dad
- D. because owners feed them

4. At what age can a female dog start having babies?

- A. three years old
- B. at least six months old
- C. anytime
- D. after its first birthday

5. Where's the best place to pat a dog you don't know very well?

A. on the head

B. on the tummy

C. on the face

D. on the shoulders

6. How many breeds of dog are there?

A. around 250

B. around 300

C. around 400

D. around 550

7. Why do puppies chew things?

A. they're naturally mischievous

B. it helps digest their food

C. it soothes their gums during teething

D. it is just a habit

8. What animal are all dogs descended from?

A. the grey wolf

B. the jackal

C. the coyote

D. the hyena

Check your answers on page 80.

did you know?

Queen Elizabeth II of Great Britain is a huge puppy fan! Her love affair with dogs began as a child when her father, King George VI, bought a corgi called Dookie. Since then she has owned at least 30 pups.

Dribbly and Delicious

Want to win your pup's heart forever? Bake it a batch of gourmet doggy treats! This yummy pet recipe will have your hound howling for more every time you get cooking.

You will need

- A little olive oil for greasing
- ½ lb. (250 g) unsalted peanut butter
- 1 cup (250 ml) skimmed milk
- ½ lb. (250 g) wholewheat flour
- 1 tablespoon baking powder
- Cookie cutter

Makes 24 doggy bites

1 Preheat the oven to 375°F (190°C). Dip a piece paper towel in a little olive oil, and then grease a flat baking tray.

2 Put the peanut butter into a mixing bowl, and then use a wooden spoon to stir in the milk. In another bowl, blend the flour and baking powder together.

3 Add some of the flour mixture into the peanut butter and milk. Beat it in, and then gradually add more and more until everything is combined. The ingredients will form a moist, nutty dough.

4 Sprinkle some flour onto a clean kitchen counter, and then knead the dough until it's soft. Roll it flat with a rolling pin, turning it regularly so that it doesn't stick.

5 Use cookie cutters to press biscuit shapes out of the dough. You could press out hearts, stars, or even bones. Put each doggy bite onto the baking tray.

6 Put the doggy bites into the oven to bake. This should take around 15 minutes. When they're ready, the treats will have turned a golden brown. Leave the bites to cool fully before feeding one to your lucky pup!

Too Cute!

Because I'm worth it!

CHAPTER 8

Puppy Love

When it comes to sweet gestures, no one can outdo a doggy. Who else would greet you with a sloppy hello lick, run around in excited circles, and thump its tail at the very mention of going out together? Aww... it really is a case of puppy love!

My Puppy Pal

These are your very own puppy pages! Write about your special pet.
It could be a real dog or a pooch you'd love to play with.

Name: ....

Boy or girl: ....

Age: ....

Fur color: ....

Eye color: ....

Stick a picture of your
puppy pal here.

Unusual markings: ....

....

....

The things it does that make
me laugh: ....

....

....

....

....

Breed: ....

Favorite toy: ....

Favorite food: ....

Five words to describe my puppy:
1. ....
2. ....
3. ....
4. ....
5. ....

What makes my puppy special: ....
....
....

Draw a picture of your puppy pal here.

Woofy Words

"It's raining cats and dogs!" "I'm dog-tired,"
"You give a dog a bad name".... Pups are such an important part of
our lives they've inspired a whole host of canine catchphrases.
Can you match all the phrases to their meanings?

1 It's a shaggy dog story.

2 Let sleeping dogs lie.

3 That's the tail wagging the dog!

4 You can't teach an old dog new tricks.

5 I'm like a dog with two tails.

6 Every dog has its day.

7 Why keep a dog and bark yourself?

8 I'm going to see a man about a dog.

A Why do a job that someone else could do for you?

B Things are the wrong way around. Something small is in charge of something much too important.

C I'm going somewhere, but I don't want to tell you where.

D I'm completely thrilled!

E It's much wiser to let things be.

F Your time will come.

G After a while, it's too late to change the way someone does something.

H This joke takes ages to tell, and the ending is pointless.

Check your answers on page 80.

75

Utterly Adorable!

This photo album is packed full of puppy pics! Look at each delectable doggy snap, and then think up a caption to write underneath it. The first picture has been labelled to get you started.

Because pets love selfies, too!

....
....
....

....
....
....

....
....
....

Perhaps the most loyal dog ever was Greyfriars Bobby. After its master died in 1858, the devoted Skye terrier slept on his grave for 14 years. There's a life-size statue of the pup near the entrance to Greyfriars churchyard, in Edinburgh, Scotland.

In the Dog House

Every dog needs somewhere comfy to curl up at the end of the day.
Use these pages to sketch your own designer kennel. Outline the
shape of the doggy den, decorate the walls, and then sketch what
it's like inside. When you've drawn your puppy paradise,
color it. Night, night, puppy dog!

Custom kennels

Does your pooch have a
taste for beautiful blankets,
cashmere cushions, or bone-
print wallpaper? Think of some
cool creature comforts to add
to your dream doggy kennel,
and then list them here:

....
....
....
....
....
....
....

Answers

Pages 10-11
Magical Mix-ups
1. E
2. F
3. D
4. C
5. A
6. B

Pages 32-33
Picture This
1. A
2. D
3. C
4. D
5. A
6. B
7. A
8. D

Pages 52-53
Fluffy and Famous

B	K	D	P	M	A	R	T	M	E	J	C
E	A	F	O	O	D	Y	B	O	O	C	S
C	U	G	Y	S	H	X	O	Q	U	I	W
T	O	R	W	P	B	N	L	A	D	Y	G
H	L	O	Y	A	G	Y	T	Y	P	O	M
O	J	M	K	T	R	T	H	Z	Z	S	L
V	Q	I	N	N	W	Z	O	A	R	B	
E	E	T	I	V	D	A	D	Q	L	F	
N	G	R	L	J	X	Q	K	U	X	G	J
T	L	A	S	S	I	E	R	M	R	P	H
R	I	N	T	I	N	T	I	N	V	E	H
C	H	D	M	J	F	X	T	E	K	D	B

Pages 66-67
Take a Bite!
1. B
2. B
3. A
4. B
5. D
6. C
7. C
8. A

Pages 74-75
Woofy Words
1. H
2. E
3. B
4. G
5. D
6. F
7. A
8. C

THE END
WOOF!